Feeding the Coal Region
A collection of Coal Region recipes
J. Reiner

Contents

Introduction 3
History 4
Appetizers and Dips 8
Canning and Cured Meats 16
Sauces and Beverages 23
Sandwiches 29
Side Dishes and Summer Salads 34
Dinner 44
Desserts 61
For the Furry Ones 74
Recipes Inspired By and Adapted From 76
Photo Caption Sources 78
Thank You 79
Safe Minimum Temperature Chart 80
Measurements 80
Index 81

Miner in a Mine (taken by Vyacheslav Svetlichnyy)

Introduction

Thank you for picking up a copy of my cookbook, *Feeding the Coal Region!*

Whether you are a former or current Coal Region resident, a Coal Region food lover, or simply a food lover, I encourage you to test, tweak, and perfect the recipes we have grown to love. I also hope you enjoy the collection of present day photos of our beautiful surroundings. Have fun and enjoy the read!

Coal Miner in the Hands Of (taken by Vyacheslav Svetlichnyy)

History
Dr. Harold Aurand, Jr.

Millions of years ago, the area that we today know as Schuylkill County lay at the bottom of a shallow, inland sea. Plants and animals living in the water, or along the shore died and sank to the bottom. Occasionally their remains were covered by silt, which washed into the sea from nearby rivers. As this process repeated itself, these layers of silt and biological remains pushed down on each other, converting the plants and animals to coal. What made Schuylkill County special was that after this process had started underway, the Appalachian Mountains formed. The immense pressure of mountain formation bent and deformed the coal deposits. Once they had been stacked horizontally on the sea floor. Now some tipped beyond vertical. There were some places where the coal outcropped directly onto the surface, and other places, maybe only a short distance away, where the coal was buried deep underground. The pressure from the Appalachian Mountains also took our regular coal and turned it into anthracite. Northeastern Pennsylvania has the largest deposits of anthracite coal in the world.

Anthracite coal is a wonderful fuel. Almost pure carbon, it gives off more heat and creates less pollution than any other coal. Despite these advantages, neither the original Native American inhabitants, nor early European settlers made much use of coal. Because coal lands are usually not good for farming, Schuylkill County's population was low, and local forests provided more than enough firewood for everyone's heating needs.

In other parts of the United States the situation was very different. Around Philadelphia, a growing population had overwhelmed the local firewood supply by 1800. More people also meant increased demand for iron products. At the time, most smelting was done with charcoal. Thousands of acres of timber were consumed each year to produce iron. Pennsylvania was clearly ready for a fuel revolution. In the 1820s, the construction of the Schuylkill Canal made it economical to ship anthracite to a wider market. America's early industrial revolution, with millions of people living in cities, and factories shifting production from rural watermill sites to urban steam driven ones, was built on anthracite coal and the iron and steel it helped create.

When anthracite first began to be used as a major source of fuel, mining companies focused on places where the coal came near the surface. Anthracite was more quarried than mined. Later, as the outcrops were used up underground mining became normal. Working in the mines had advantages and disadvantages. For the actual miners, work was done by small teams in different parts of the mine. One worker was a skilled miner, charged with placing the explosives and blowing the coal out of the wall. Because these miners worked in different parts of the mine, there was little supervision. The miners decided for themselves where to set the explosives, prop up the roof, and what pace to work at. Many miners were paid by the ton, and considered themselves to be independent contractors, sharing with the mine owner responsibility for production. Few other jobs offered as much independence or sense of accomplishment.

At the same time, miners were often poorly paid. A lot of anthracite coal was used for home heating, so demand tended to be seasonal. Miners would work full time during part of the year, then see their hours cut as demand slackened. Some individual mines, desperate to earn more money, continued to produce even when demand was low. This overproduction led to falling prices, which kept wages low. A second problem was that working underground and setting off explosions is inherently dangerous work. Many miners lost time and wages after injuries, and a bread-winners death could devastate a whole family. It isn't surprising that the first anthracite miners' union, the Workingmen's Benevolent Association, focused on passing mine safety laws, and a sliding scale that tied wages to the price of coal. The anthracite coal mining industry was the first one in the United States to be governed by a comprehensive set of safety laws.

Mine owners recruited workers from a variety of sources. The most useful were people with experience working in coal mines, like many Welsh immigrants. Others had to be trained, often by progressing from unskilled workers up through the ranks. Usually, the bulk of the people who came to Schuylkill County reflected the groups who were coming into the United States in general at that time. This meant Irish Catholics in the years before the Civil War, and Southern and Eastern Europeans afterward. Local Pennsylvania Dutch farmers were also brought in, while the county's small African-American population tended to work outside the mines.

As anyone can imagine, coming to a new country and starting in on a new type of work could be very disorienting. Many immigrants sought comfort in socializing with their fellows. Groups like the Catholic Church helped make this possible. They allowed immigrants to set up national parishes, where services could be in their own languages and they could continue to celebrate traditional feast and saint days. Social groups like the Ancient Order of Hibernians and Knights of Lithuania were also set up along ethnic lines. These helped preserve many traditions from the old world.

Heaps of Coal (taken by Rasta777)

A second, although unfortunate, factor that helped maintain ethnic traditions was that the anthracite coal industry began to decline after World War I. Oil had become cheaper as a source of heat, and coked bituminous coal took over for many industrial uses. Many Schuylkill County residents moved away, but more importantly, few newcomers came in. Why move into an area with a declining job base? By the 1950s, the people who moved away were settling in new suburban communities. Assimilation and intermarriage had taken away the need for ethnic churches and social organizations, so new, more inclusive institutions were built. Here we had no need for new institutions. The old ones were still standing, and large enough to accommodate our needs. Even today, long after intermarriage and just simply learning to get along has blurred ethnic lines, Schuylkill County to continues to enjoy traditions that have disappeared from many other places.

Recently, although the coal industry has not revived, Schuylkill County has started to become a destination for immigrants again. People from South America and Asia have begun to add to our rich tradition of diversity. This cookbook is a record of the foods people brought with them, and ones they developed here in Schuylkill County. Let's hope the all continue to be eaten and enjoyed, and maybe even new ones added to the regional menu.

Saint Nicholas Breaker, Mahanoy City (submitted by R. Thomas Berner)
Constructed in March 1931, the Saint Nicholas Breaker was capable of processing 12,000 ton of anthracite daily, [1]

Appetizers and Dips

Don't go bacon my heart!

Bacon Wrapped Water Chestnuts
- 2 cans of whole water chestnuts (drained), 1 ½ cups of soy sauce, 1 cup of brown sugar, 1 pound of bacon (cut in half)
- Soak water chestnuts in soy sauce for 1 hour, roll in brown sugar, wrap with bacon, roll in brown sugar again, and bake for 30 minutes at 400 degrees

Buffalo Chicken Dip
- 1 block of cream cheese (softened), 1 large can of white meat chicken (drained), 1 cup of hot sauce, 1 cup of ranch dressing, 2 cups of shredded mozzarella cheese
- Combine all ingredients, pour into a baking dish, and bake for 20 minutes at 350 degrees
- Serve with tortilla chips, celery, and carrots

Spinach and Water Chestnut Dip
- 1 can diced water chestnuts, 1 package frozen spinach (thawed and drained), 1 block of cream cheese (softened), 16 ounces of sour cream, 1 packet of ranch dip mix, 2 cups of shredded sharp cheddar cheese
- Combine all ingredients, pour into a baking dish, and bake for 30 minutes at 350 degrees
- Serve with lime tortilla chips and crostini

Taco Dip (shared by D. Riotto)
- 1 block of cream cheese (softened), 1 packet of taco seasoning, 1 pound of ground meat (browned and drained), 1 can of diced tomatoes, 2 cups of shredded taco blend cheese
- Spread cream cheese in the bottom of a pie dish, combine ground meat, taco seasoning, and diced tomatoes over medium heat until heated through, pour over cream cheese, top with shredded cheese, and bake for 20 minutes at 350 degrees
- Serve with tortilla chips

Bacon and Swiss Dip
- ½ pound of bacon (browned and crumbled), 1 block of cream cheese (softened), ½ cup of mayonnaise, 1 teaspoon of dijon mustard, 1 teaspoon of horseradish, 2 cups of shredded Swiss cheese
- Combine all ingredients and bake for 20 minutes at 350 degrees
- Serve with crostini, celery, and carrots

Beer and Cheddar Dip
- ½ Pound of bacon (browned and crumbled), 8 ounces of beer, 1 block of cream cheese (softened), 2 cloves of garlic (minced), 2 tablespoons of flour, 2 tablespoons of butter, ½ teaspoon of ground mustard, 4 cups of shredded cheddar cheese, 1 tablespoon of hot sauce
- Melt butter over medium heat, stir in the garlic, stir in the flour, and stir in the remaining ingredients until melted and smooth
- Serve with soft or hard pretzels

Maple Bacon Deviled Eggs [1]
- ¼ pound of bacon, 2 tablespoons of brown sugar, 1 tablespoon plus 1 teaspoon of maple syrup, 1 dozen hard boiled eggs, ¾ cup of mayonnaise, 1 tablespoon plus 1 teaspoon of dijon mustard, ¼ teaspoon of ground cayenne pepper, salt and pepper
- Combine 2 tablespoons of brown sugar, 1 teaspoon of maple syrup, and 1 teaspoon of dijon mustard, brush over bacon, bake at 350 degrees until crisp, cool, and crumble
- Cut hardboiled eggs in half, scoop out egg yolks, and combine with the remaining ingredients (reserving bacon)
- Spoon into hardboiled egg white halves and sprinkle with bacon

Bleenies
- 3 potatoes (grated), 1 small onion (grated), 1 egg, 3 tablespoons of flour, salt and pepper
- Combine potatoes and onion, drain, and stir in remaining ingredients
- Form a rounded handful, flatten, fry until golden brown on both sides, and drain on paper towels

There is nothing quite like a bleenie from a summer block party and I found that the bleenies will maintain their shape well if the grated onions and potatoes are drained before they are combined with the remaining ingredients.

Cheese ball ₃
- 2 blocks of cream cheese (softened), 2 cups of shredded sharp cheddar cheese, 3 tablespoons of diced pimentos, 2 tablespoons of dried and minced onion, 2 tablespoons of chopped red pepper, 2 tablespoons of hot sauce, 2 cups of chopped pecans
- Combine all ingredients for the exception of the chopped pecans, form into 2 balls, roll in chopped pecans, and chill
- Serve with crackers, celery, and carrots

Bread Bowl Spinach Dip
- 1 round loaf of pumpernickel bread, 2 cups of sour cream, 1 packet of ranch dressing mix, 1 package of frozen spinach (thawed and drained)
- Hollow bread loaf and cube hollowed out section of bread
- Combine remaining ingredients and spoon into hollow bread loaf
- Serve with bread cubes, celery, and carrots

Crab Stuffed Mushrooms

- 16 ounces of whole button mushrooms, 6 ounce can of lump crab meat (drained), 2 tablespoons of butter, 2 tablespoons of cream cheese (softened), 1 shallot, 2 teaspoons of minced garlic, ¼ cup of bread crumbs
- Remove stems from mushroom caps and dice
- Sauté stems, shallots, and garlic in butter over medium heat until tender and stir in remaining ingredients
- Fill mushroom caps with mixture, top with grated parmesan cheese, and bake for 20 minutes at 425 degrees

Cheese board [4]

- Seedless grapes, dried apricots, fig preserves, rosemary crackers, 1 wedge of gruyere cheese, 1 wedge of sharp cheddar, 1 log of cranberry goat cheese, 1 wedge of blue cheese
- Center fig preserves on platter and arrange remaining ingredients

Irish Cheese

- 16 ounces of grated Irish cheddar cheese, 4 ounces of cream cheese (softened), ½ cup of beer, 1 clove of garlic (minced), 2 teaspoons of ground mustard, 1 teaspoon of paprika
- Puree all ingredients until smooth
- Serve with apple slices, bread, and carrots

Tuscarora State Park, Barnesville
Founded in 1971, Tuscarora State Park covers an area of 1,618 acres, [2]

Strawberry Bruschetta [2]

- 1 cup of strawberries (diced), 2 tablespoons of sugar, 1 tablespoon of balsamic vinegar, ½ cup of mascarpone cheese, ¼ cup of powdered sugar
- Combine strawberries, 2 tablespoons of sugar, and 1 tablespoon of balsamic vinegar, rest for 45 minutes

- Drizzle crostini with olive oil and bake at 425 degrees until crisp
- Combine mascarpone cheese and powdered sugar, spread on cooled crostini, top with strawberries, and basil

Traditional Bruschetta

- 2 garlic cloves (minced), 2 tablespoons of olive oil, ¼ cup of grated parmesan cheese, 3 cups of tomatoes (chopped), 1/3 cup of basil (chopped), 2 tablespoons of balsamic vinegar, ½ teaspoon of salt, 1 teaspoon of pepper

- Drizzle crostini with olive oil and bake at 425 until lightly crisp
- Combine remaining ingredients and spread on crostini

Mushroom Bruschetta

- 2 tablespoons of olive oil, ¼ cup of grated parmesan cheese, 1 pound of mushrooms (sliced), 6 sprigs of thyme, salt and pepper

- Drizzle crostini with olive oil and bake at 425 until lightly crisp
- Combine remaining ingredients, bake at 375 degrees until tender, and spread on crostini

Waterfall at Sweet Arrow Lake County Park, Pine Grove
The Schuylkill County Board of Commissioners acquired the property in 2001 and the site is comprised of 60 acres of water and 123 acres of land. [3]

Canning and Meats
Turn it up, this is my jam!

Growing up, my Nanny's basement was filled with an assortment of canned fruits, vegetables, jams, sauces, and beverages. I was often sent down to the basement to gather a jar of stewed tomatoes to compliment macaroni and cheese or a jar of jam to spread on toast.

Hot Bologna
- 2 rings of bologna (halved and sliced), 2 tablespoons of crushed red pepper, ½ teaspoon of cayenne pepper, 1/4 teaspoon of salt, 2 cloves of garlic (omitted if using garlic bologna), 1 teaspoon of sugar (omitted if using honey bologna), 3 cups of white vinegar, 1.5 cups of water
- Combine water and vinegar
- Place remaining ingredients into a large jar, pour in enough vinegar mixture to cover, shake, and refrigerate

Hot bologna made with honey bologna is the perfect combination of spicy and sweet!

Dandelion Jelly
- 1 quart of dandelion flowers (stems and greens removed), 2 tablespoons of lemon juice, zest of 1 lemon, 5 ½ cups of sugar, 1 package of dry pectin
- Boil dandelion flowers for 10 minutes, drain, and reserve 3 cups of juice
- Bring 3 cups of juice, lemon juice, zest, and pectin to a boil, stir in sugar, and boil for 2 minutes
- Can and seal

Apple or Pear Butter
- 6 pounds of apples or pears (peeled, cored, and chopped), 4 cups of sugar, 3 teaspoons of cinnamon, ¼ teaspoon of salt
- Combine all ingredients in crock pot, simmer on high for 1 hour, low for 8 hours, and uncovered for 1 hour
- Can and seal

Sweet Pepper Relish [5]
- 6 cups of tomatoes (diced), 6 cups of red peppers (diced), 6 cups of sugar, 2 tablespoons of salt, 3 cups of white vinegar, 3 onions (diced), 2 jalapenos (diced), 2 packs of liquid pectin
- Bring all ingredients expect pectin to boil, reduce heat and simmer for 2.5 hours, stir in pectin, and boil for 2 minutes
- Can and seal

Sweet and Spicy Pickles [6]
- 3 pounds of pickling cucumbers (sliced), 2 onions (sliced), ½ cup of pickling salt, 6 cups of water, 3 cups of white vinegar, 1.5 cups of apple cider vinegar, 4 cups of sugar, 2 tablespoons of mustard seeds, ½ teaspoon of turmeric, 4 cloves, 9 tablespoons minced garlic, 20 dried cayenne peppers
- Combine cucumbers, onions, pickling salt, and water in a bowl, rest for 2 hours, drain, and rinse
- Bring remaining ingredients to a boil, remove from heat, stir in cucumbers, onions, and ladle into jars
- Can and seal

Candied Jalapeños [7]
- 3 pounds of fresh jalapenos (sliced), 2 cups of apple cider vinegar, 6 cups of white sugar, ½ teaspoon of turmeric, ½ teaspoon of celery seed, 3 teaspoons of garlic powder, 1 teaspoon of ground cayenne pepper
- Bring all ingredients except jalapenos to boil, reduce heat and simmer for 5 minutes, stir in jalapenos, and simmer for an additional 5 minutes
- Ladle jalapenos into jars, boil liquid for an additional 5 minutes, and pour into jars
- Can and seal

Scrapple 8
- 1 pound of breakfast sausage, 1 pound of bratwurst links (casing removed), 3 cups of water, ¼ teaspoon of salt, ¼ teaspoon of pepper, ¼ teaspoon of onion powder, ¼ teaspoon of garlic powder, ¼ teaspoon of thyme, ¼ teaspoon of sage, ¼ teaspoon ground cayenne pepper, 1.5 cups of corn meal, 4 tablespoons of butter (melted)
- Combine breakfast sausage, bratwurst, and water over medium high heat until cooked through, blend until smooth, return to pot, stir in remaining ingredients, and simmer over medium heat until thickened.
- Pour into loaf pans, chill overnight, slice, and pan fry until golden brown

Hash 9
- 1 onion (chopped), 2 pounds corned beef (cubed), 3 potatoes (cubed), 3 tablespoons vegetable oil
- Sauté onion in oil over medium high heat until tender, stir in potatoes and corned beef, and allow to fry until crust forms

Hash drizzled with maple syrup is wonderful!

Old Route 61, Centralia (taken by S. Cicecro)
In the mid 1980's, the fire began to surface near Route 61, causing ground subsidence and emitting steam. Route 61 was relocated and a this one mile stretch was bypassed. [4]

Corn Cob Jelly
- 12 corn cobs (kernels removed), 1 package of fruit pectin, 3 ½ cups of sugar, 4 drops of yellow food coloring
- Boil corn cobs for 10 minutes, discard corn cobs, reserve 3 ½ cups of water, stir in pectin, bring to boil, stir in sugar and food coloring, bring to boil, skim off foam, and pour into jars
- Can and seal

Rhubarb Jam
- 4 cups of rhubarb (chopped), 4 cups of sugar, 1 jar of maraschino cherries (10 ounces, diced and undrained), 1 can of crushed pineapple (8 ounces, undrained), 1 package of raspberry jello (6 ounces)
- Simmer rhubarb, sugar, and cherries for 10 minutes, stir in crushed pineapple, remove from heat, and stir in raspberry jello
- Can and refrigerate

Chow Chow [10]
- 5 pounds of tomatoes (diced), 2 pounds of carrots (diced), 10 green peepers (diced), 10 onions (diced), 2 heads of cauliflower (diced), 1 ½ quarts of pickles, 1 cup of lima beans (softened), 1 cup of corn, 2 stalks of celery (diced), ½ cup of canning salt, 2 cups of vinegar, 5 cups of sugar, 8 cups of cold water, 1 tablespoon of pepper, 2 teaspoons of turmeric
- Combine vegetables and salt, allow to rest overnight, and drain
- Combine vegetables with remaining ingredients and boil until tender
- Can and seal

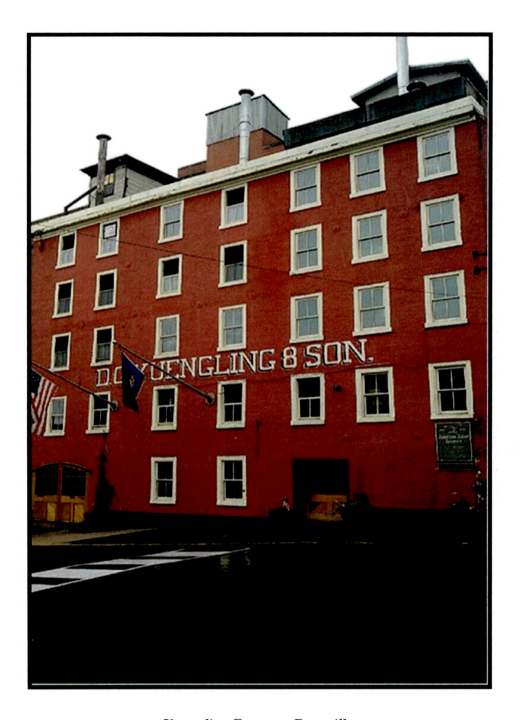

Yuengling Brewery, Pottsville
Established in 1829, D.G. Yuengling & Son is America's Oldest Brewery, 5

Sauces and Beverages
O no! I bought beer instead of milk… again!

Hamburger and Hot Dog Chili Sauce

- 1 pound of ground beef, water to cover, 1 onion (diced), 1 cup of ketchup, 2 tablespoons of Worcestershire sauce, 1 tablespoon of brown sugar, 1 tablespoon of mustard, 2 teaspoons of chili powder, 2 teaspoons of minced garlic, 1 teaspoon of dried minced onion, 2 teaspoons of red pepper flakes, ½ teaspoon of ground cayenne pepper, ¼ teaspoon of cumin, ½ teaspoon of salt, ½ teaspoon of pepper

- Combine all ingredients and boil until all water evaporates

Balsamic Dressing

- ¼ teaspoon of salt, 1/8 teaspoon of pepper, ¼ cup of diced red onion, 2 tablespoons of sugar, 2 tablespoons of balsamic vinegar, ¼ cup of olive oil
- Combine all ingredients and serve over spring mix

Caesar Dressing

- ¼ cup of olive oil, 2 teaspoons of minced garlic, 4 teaspoons of lemon juice, ½ teaspoon of Worcestershire sauce, ¼ teaspoon pepper, 1 anchovy
- Blend all ingredients and serve over romaine lettuce sprinkled with parmesan cheese and croutons

Rock Covered Bridge over Swatara Creek, Pine Grove
The Rock Covered Bridge crosses the Little Swatara Creek, is 56 feet long, and was built in 1870, [6]

Pizza Hot Sauce [11]
- 3 cups of tomato sauce, 3 pickled banana peppers (minced), 4 tablespoons of onions (minced), 4 tablespoons of red pepper flakes, 1 tablespoon of vinegar, 1 tablespoon of sugar, 2 cloves of garlic (minced), ½ tablespoon of salt
- Bring all ingredients to a boil and simmer for 5 minutes

Many pizza places in the Coal Region serve their pizza with a spicy dipping sauce, which is typically placed in a dipping cup in the center of the pizza. It is especially tasty when served with a sweet sauce pizza!

Hot Bacon Dressing on Spinach Salad
- 5 slices of bacon (diced), 2 eggs, 2 ½ tablespoons of vinegar, 1 cup of water, ¼ cup of sweet cream, ½ tablespoon of salt, 2 tablespoons of sugar
- Fry bacon, remove from pan, and whisk in remaining ingredients
- Pour over spinach, hardboiled egg, and red onion salad

Horseradish and Red Beet Sauce
- 1 pound of beets (boiled), 2 ounces of horseradish, 2 tablespoons of vinegar, 1 teaspoon of sugar, 1 teaspoon of salt, 1/3 cup of water
- Grate beets and horseradish, stir in remaining ingredients, bring to boil, remove from heat, and cool before serving

Boilo
- 3 oranges (quartered), 2 lemons (quartered), 1/2 cup of raisins, 4 ounces of honey, 2 sticks of cinnamon, ½ teaspoon of ground cloves, 12 ounces of ginger ale
- Combine all ingredients, simmer for 15 -20 minutes, strain, and stir in 1 bottle of whiskey

Apple Cider Boilo (shared by Val Shertzer)
- 3 red delicious apples (optional), 1 gallon of apple cider, ½ gallon of apple juice (concentrate preferred), 2 tablespoons of vanilla extract, ½ cup of sugar, 1/3 cup of brown sugar, 4 cinnamon sticks, 750ml Four Queens whiskey
- Combine all ingredients for the exception of whiskey, simmer for 2 hours, cool overnight, strain, and stir in whiskey

Boilo makes a wonderful gift, is warming on a cold winter's night, and many swear that drinking it will alleviate cold and flu symptoms. We like to have a warm glass of boilo with a cold beer to toast special occasions!

Red Sangria
- 2 bottles of red wine, 1 cup of brandy, ½ cup of triple sec, 1 ½ cups of orange juice, 1 cup of pomegranate juice, ½ cup of sugar, 1 orange (sliced), ½ cup of blackberries
- Combine all ingredients and serve

White Sangria
- 1 bottle of white wine, 1/3 cup of sugar, ¼ cup of brandy, 2 tablespoons of triple sec, 1 cup of ginger ale, ½ of a honey dew melon (sliced)
- Combine all ingredients and serve

Apple Sangria [12]
- 1 bottle of white wine, 3 granny smith apples (sliced), 6 cups of apple cider, 1 cup of caramel vodka
- Combine all ingredients and serve

Garfield Square in Spring, Pottsville (taken by S. Cicero)
The Soldiers's Monument of Schuylkill County was dedicated in 1897. Many residents from the Coal Region enlisted in Pottsville and joined regiments organized there, 7

Wells Fargo Bank, Pottsville (Former Schuylkill Trust)
Located at the corner of West Market and Centre Street and was built in 1924, 8

Sandwiches
Chop it like it's hot!

Stewed Burgers (shared by D. Riotto)
- ½ cup of vinegar, 1 cup of water, 2 onions (sliced), ½ jalapeno (diced), 1 teaspoon of salt, ½ teaspoon of pepper, dash of ground cayenne pepper, 3 tablespoons of sugar, 2 tablespoons of mustard, 6 tablespoons of Worcestershire sauce, 1 cup of ketchup, ¼ cup of butter, 12 cooked hamburgers
- Bring all ingredients to boil over medium high heat, add in hamburgers, reduce heat, and simmer 45 minutes

Ham and Swiss Sticky Buns [23]
- 12 Hawaiian rolls, ½ pound of ham, ½ pound of Swiss cheese, 1 stick of butter, 1 tablespoon of dried minced onion, 1.5 tablespoons of poppy seeds, 1/3 cup of brown sugar, 2 tablespoons of Worcestershire sauce, 1.5 tablespoons of mustard
- Assemble ham and cheese sandwiches, bring remaining ingredients to boil, pour over sandwiches, and bake for 25 minutes at 350 degrees

Sausage and Peppers
- 3 hot Italian sausages, 3 sweet Italian sausages, 2 onions, 1 red pepper, 1 green pepper, olive oil, 1 tablespoon of tomato paste, 3 cloves of minced garlic, ½ cup of chicken stock
- Pan fry the sausages in olive oil over medium high heat until cooked through and brown, remove from pan and set aside, sauté onions and peppers until tender, stir in tomato paste, garlic, chicken stock, and season with salt and pepper
- Serve on rolls

Lobster Cheesesteak, [24]
- 2 lobster tails (meat removed and chopped), 1.5 pounds of ribeye steak, 1 onion, 6 tablespoons of butter, 2 tablespoons of flour, 2.5 cups of milk, ½ pound of American cheese, rolls
- Melt 2 tablespoons of butter, stir in 2 tablespoons of flour, stir in milk, stir in American cheese, and season with salt and pepper
- Thinly slice ribeye steak and sauté with onion in canola oil until tender
- Sauté the lobster in 4 tablespoons of butter until cooked through
- Pile steak and onions on roll, tops with lobster and cheese sauce

BBQ
- 1 pound of ground meat (browned and drained), 1 onion (chopped and cooked), 1.5 tablespoons vinegar, 3 tablespoons brown sugar, 1.5 teaspoons mustard, ¾ cup of ketchup, salt and pepper, rolls
- Combine all ingredient, simmer for 15 minutes over medium high heat, and serve on rolls

Lofty Tunnel, Ringtown (taken by N. Cicero)
Opened in 1854, the Lofty Tunnel is located in Kline Township, underneath Interstate 81. The Lofty Tunnel linked the Little Schuylkill Railroad with Milton at the foot of Broad Mountain,[9]

Brown Sugar Glazed and Stuffed Bacon Burgers
- 3 tablespoons of brown sugar, 1.5 teaspoons of paprika, ½ teaspoon of garlic powder, ½ teaspoon of cumin, ¼ teaspoon of ground cayenne pepper, ¼ teaspoon of salt, ¼ teaspoon of pepper, 1 ½ pounds of ground meat, ½ cup of shredded sharp cheddar cheese, ½ pound of bacon (cooked and chopped)
- Form ground meat into 8 patties, place an equivalent amount of cheese and bacon in the center of 4 of the patties, place the remaining patties over the cheese/bacon patties, and seal the edges
- Combine seasonings, roll stuffed hamburgers in seasonings, grill, and serve on rolls

Pimento Cheese, Bacon, and Fried Tomato Sandwiches [13]
- 2 jars of diced pimentos (drained), 20 ounces grated sharp cheddar, 1 block of cream cheese (softened), ½ cup of mayonnaise, 1 fresh jalapeno (seeded and diced), 4 tomatoes (sliced and sprinkled with salt and pepper), 1 teaspoon salt, pepper, 1.5 cups of flour, ½ teaspoon of cayenne pepper, ½ teaspoon of paprika, 3 eggs, ¼ cup of buttermilk, 2 cups of panko bread crumbs, ¼ cup of parmesan cheese, vegetable oil, ½ pounds bacon (fried), lettuce, bread
- Combine cream cheese, pimentos, grated sharp cheddar, mayonnaise, and jalapenos in mixer until combined
- In a bowl, combine flour, cayenne pepper, paprika, ¼ teaspoon of salt and pepper. In another bowl, combine eggs and buttermilk. In another bowl, combine panko, ½ teaspoon salt, pepper, and parmesan cheese
- Dip tomatoes in flour mixture, egg mixture, and then in panko mixture, fry in oil until golden brown, and drain on paper towels
- Spread toasted bread with pimento cheese, top with lettuce, bacon, and fried tomato

Side Dishes and Summer Salads
Thyme to turnip the beet!

Filling (shared by T. Kinsley)
- 5 pounds of mashed potatoes, 5 celery ribs (diced), 1 onion (diced), 1 stick of butter, 5 slices of toast (cubed and soaked briefly in chicken broth), garlic salt, poultry seasoning, parsley, salt and pepper
- Sauté celery and onion in butter until tender and lightly browned, sprinkle with seasonings, toss all ingredients, pour into a baking dish, make divots on top with the back of a spoon, pour broth into divots, and bake at 350 degrees until golden

My first Manager taught me many things including how to make her filling shortly after I married my Husband. It is a wonderful, easy, and traditional recipe, which can be made throughout the year! A helpful tip is - the longer you allow your vegetable mixture to cook, the darker it will be come, which results in a darker filling.

Roasted Brussels Sprouts
- 2 pounds of brussels sprouts, ½ pound of bacon (cooked and crumbled) drizzle of olive oil, salt and pepper
- Combine all ingredients and roast for 25 minutes at 425 degrees

Try drizzling the roasted Brussels Sprouts with balsamic vinegar and brown sugar!

Green Bean Casserole 25
- 1 pound of fresh green beans (boiled for 2 minutes), 1 tablespoon of flour, 2 tablespoons of butter, 2 teaspoons of minced garlic, 1 pound of mushrooms (sliced and sautéed), ¼ teaspoon of thyme, ¼ teaspoon of nutmeg, ½ cup of milk, ½ cup of heavy cream, 2 teaspoons of Worcestershire sauce, ¾ cup of fried onions, salt and pepper
- Melt butter, stir in flour, stir in remaining ingredients, top with fried onions, and bake for 15 minutes at 350 degrees

Ramen Slaw
- 1 pound of broccoli slaw, 3 tablespoons of sesame seeds, 1 cup of almonds (sliced), 3 green onions (diced), 1 package of chicken ramen noodles (dry), ¼ cup of oil, 3 tablespoons of vinegar, ¼ cup of sugar, salt and pepper
- Combine all ingredients and refrigerate until ready to serve

Macaroni Salad
- 1 pound of elbow noodles (cooked), 1 red pepper (diced), 1 green pepper (diced), ½ red onion (diced), 1 cup of carrots (shredded), 2 ribs of celery (diced), 1 can of sweetened condensed milk, ½ cup of vinegar, ¼ cup of sugar, 2 cups of ranch dressing or mayonnaise, salt and pepper
- Combine all ingredients and refrigerate for 8 hours before serving

Potato Salad
- 2 pounds of potatoes (cubed and boiled), ½ pound of bacon (cooked and crumbled), 4 ribs of celery (diced), ½ onion (diced), 1/3 cup sweet relished (drained), 1 ¼ cups ranch dressing or mayonnaise, 2 teaspoons of sugar, 2 teaspoons of celery seeds, 2 teaspoons of apple cider vinegar, 2 teaspoons of mustard, 1 teaspoon of salt, 2 eggs (hardboiled and diced)
- Combine all ingredients and refrigerate until ready to serve

Baked German Potato Salad [10]
- 1 bunch of celery (diced), 2 onions (diced), 12 potatoes (boiled and cubed), 1 pound of smoked bacon (fried and drained), ½ pound of Swiss cheese, 6 eggs (boiled, diced), 2 raw eggs, 1 cup of sweet wine, 6 tablespoons of flour, 2 tablespoons of sugar, ½ cup of vinegar
- Combine flour, sugar, raw eggs, wine, vinegar, and ½ cup of water into a paste, stir paste into 2 quarts of warm water, stir in remaining ingredients, and bake until golden at 350 degrees

Honey Glazed Carrots
- 2 pounds of baby carrots (boiled until tender), 1 teaspoon of salt, ½ stick of butter, 5 tablespoons of honey, 3 tablespoons of brown sugar, 1 tablespoon of lemon juice, fresh parsley, salt and pepper
- Combine all ingredients and sauté until warmed through and coated

South Centre Street, Pottsville
The Schuylkill County Municipal Authority was formed in 1961, [10]
The mansion on the left, known as the Sheafer Building, which is located at 325 South Centre Street was built in 1893, [11]

Broccoli Salad
- 2 bunches of broccoli (diced), 1 red onion (diced), ½ cup of raisins, 1 pound of bacon (cooked and crumbled), 1 cup of ranch dressing or mayonnaise, ½ cup of sugar, 2 tablespoons of apple cider vinegar
- Combine all ingredients and refrigerate until ready to serve

Bow Tie Pasta Salad
- 1 box of bowtie pasta (cooked), ½ cucumber (diced), 1 cup of cherry tomatoes (halved), 5 green onions (diced), 1 green pepper (diced), 1 red pepper (diced), 1 tablespoon salad supreme seasoning, ¼ cup parmesan cheese, 1 cup Italian dressing (3/4 cup vegetable oil, ¼ cup apple cider vinegar, 1 teaspoon minced garlic, 2 teaspoons sugar, 1 teaspoon salt, ¼ teaspoon pepper, 1 teaspoon parmesan cheese)
- Combine all ingredients and refrigerate until ready to serve

Red Beet Eggs [26]
- 8 eggs (hardboiled and peeled), 2 cans of sliced beets, 1 onion (sliced), 1 cup of sugar, ¾ cup of apple cider vinegar, ½ teaspoon of salt, ½ teaspoon of pepper, 3 bay leaves, 12 cloves, ¼ teaspoon of cinnamon

- Place eggs, onions, beets in a glass bowl, boil beet juice, bay leaves, vinegar, sugar, salt and pepper for 5 minutes, and pour over egg mixture
- Refrigerate for 2 days before serving

Collard Greens [14]
- 1 large bag of collard greens (boiled for 15 minutes and drained), ½ pound of bacon (cooked and crumbled), 1 box of chicken broth, 1 jalapeno pepper (diced), 1 teaspoon of minced garlic, salt and pepper
- Combine all ingredients in crock pot and cook on low for 4 hours

Pineapple Bake (shared by D. Riotto)
- 1 large can of crushed pineapple, 8 slices of white bread (cubed), 1 cup of sugar, 4 eggs
- Combine all ingredients and bake for 1 hour at 350 degrees

Colcannon
- 8 potatoes (cooked and mashed with butter and milk), 1 head of cabbage (grated and sautéed in butter), 1 cup of kale (sliced and sautéed in butter), 6 scallions (chopped)
- Combine all ingredients and season with salt and pepper

Hash Brown Casserole
- 2 pounds of shredded potatoes (frozen), ½ cup of butter (melted), 1 can of cream of chicken soup, 1 pint of sour cream, 1 onion (diced), 2 cups of sharp cheddar cheese (grated), 1 teaspoon of salt, ½ teaspoon of pepper, dash of tabasco sauce

- Combine all ingredients, top with corn flakes drizzled with butter, and bake for 45 minutes at 350 degrees

Hash brown casserole is also wonderful topped with frosted corn flakes!

Green Beans and Tomatoes [10]
- 1 onion (diced), 1 pound of green beans (trimmed), 1 clove of garlic (chopped), ½ teaspoon of dried mint, 1 tablespoon of parsley, 1 teaspoon of fennel, ½ cup of tomato sauce, ¼ cup of water, salt and pepper
- Sautee onions and green beans in butter until tender, stir in remaining ingredients, and simmer for 30 minutes

Hrudka (Easter Cheese) [15]
- 12 eggs (beaten), 1 quart of milk, 1 cup of sugar, 1 teaspoon of salt, 1 teaspoon of cinnamon
- Combine all ingredients in saucepan over medium-high heat and whisk constantly until curds form, drain into 5 layers of cheesecloth, twist, tie, and hang overnight

Traditional Cole Slaw
- 4 carrots (shredded), 1 head of cabbage (shredded), 1 cup of red cabbage (shredded), 1 cup of mayonnaise, ½ cup of sugar, 2 tablespoons of apple cider vinegar, salt and pepper
- Combine all ingredients and refrigerate overnight

French Onion Casserole [17]
- 2 tablespoons of butter, 4 large sweet onions, 1 can of cream of mushroom soup, 2/3 cup of milk, 1 teaspoon of Worcestershire sauce, sliced baguette, 2 cups of shredded Swiss cheese
- Sauté onion in butter until tender, stir in remaining ingredients, pour into a casserole dish, top with bread, shredded Swiss, and bake for 30 minutes at 350 degrees

**Thomaston Freight and Passenger Station, Heckscherville
(taken by S. Cicero)**
The Thomaston Freight and Passenger Station is located in the Heckscherville Valley. It was owned by Mine Hill and Schuylkill Haven Railroad until 1864, at which time it was leased to the Philadelphia and Reading Railroad, [12]

Paska 16
- 2 packages of active dry yeast (dissolved in ½ cup of warm water), ½ cup of sugar (dissolved in 3 cups of warm milk), 4 cups of flour
- Combine yeast mixture, milk mixture, and flour, allow to rest for 2 hours or until doubled in size
- Stir in 6 beaten eggs, ½ cup of sugar, 1 cup of butter (softened), ½ teaspoon of lemon zest, and gradually add in 12 cups of flour
- Knead until soft, place in greased bowl and allow to rest for 2 hours or until doubled in size, punch down, and allow to rest for an additional 30 minutes
- Divide into 3 equal and rounded loaves, allow to rest for 1 hour on greased cookie sheets, brush will egg, and bake for 45 minutes at 350 degrees

Creamed Cucumbers
- 4 cucumbers (peeled and thinly sliced), 1 sweet onion (thinly sliced), 1 cup of sour cream, ¼ cup of sugar, 2 tablespoons of apple cider vinegar, 3 tablespoons of dill, salt and pepper
- Combine all ingredients and refrigerate until ready to serve

Apples and Cranberries
- 6 apples (cored and chopped), 2 teaspoons of cinnamon, ¾ cup of water, 1 cup of brown sugar, 1 ½ cups of walnuts (chopped), 2 cups of dried cranberries
- Combine all ingredients and bake at 350 degrees until tender

Dinner
The whisk wasn't the tallest, but he had amazing hair!

Halushki
- 1 bag of egg noodles (boiled), 1 stick of butter, 1 large sweet onion (sliced), ¾ teaspoons of caraway seeds, 1 head of cabbage (sliced), 1 tablespoon of brown sugar, salt and pepper
- Combine all ingredients (except egg noodles), sauté for 20 minutes/until cabbage is tender, and toss with egg noodles

Halupki (Blind Pigeons)
- 1 head of cabbage (boiled until tender and leaves separated), 1 pound of ground beef, ½ pound of ground pork, 1 ½ cups of white rice (cooked), 1 onion (diced and sautéed in ½ stick of butter until tender), 1 can of diced tomatoes, 1 can of tomato soup, paprika, salt and pepper
- Combine beef, pork, rice, and onions sautéed in butter, roll meat mixture into cabbage leaves, combine remaining ingredients, pour over pigeons, cover, and bake for 2.5 hours at 350 degrees.

Making Pigeons in a bundt pan is a little easier! (idea shared by Valerie Cascione)

Macaroni and Cheese (shared by D. Riotto)
- 1 box of elbow noodles (boiled), 4 tablespoons of flour, 4 tablespoons of butter, 1 pound of American cheese, 5 cups of milk, salt and pepper
- Melt butter, stir in flour, stir in milk, stir in cheese, salt and pepper, toss with elbow noodles, and bake at 375 degrees for 25 minutes

Chicken Noodle Soup
- 2 boneless chicken breasts, 1 cup of celery (diced), 1 cup of carrots (diced), 1 cup of onions (chopped), 2 ½ boxes of chicken broth, 2 teaspoons fresh ginger, 2 sprigs of rosemary, 2 chicken bouillon cubes, parsley, garlic salt, pepper, ½ bag of egg noodles (cooked)
- Combine all ingredients (except egg noodles), simmer until vegetables are tender and chicken is cooked, shred chicken, and stir in noodles

Nanny's Meatballs and Sauce
- Sauce: 3 small cans of tomato paste with Italian seasoning (plus 9 cans of water), 2 large cans of tomato puree (plus 1 can of water), 1 teaspoon of salt, 1 teaspoon of pepper, 2 tablespoons of Italian seasoning, 2 tablespoons of parsley, 2 teaspoons of minced garlic, 1 tablespoon of sugar, 1 pinch of baking soda
- Combine all ingredients and simmer (do not rapidly boil), stirring frequently
- Meatballs: 3 pounds of ground beef, 1 egg, 1 piece of bread (torn into small pieces), ½ teaspoon of salt, ½ teaspoon of pepper, ½ teaspoon of garlic powder, ½ cup of parmesan cheese, 1 tablespoon of parsley, 1 tablespoon of Italian seasoning, ½ cup of Italian bread crumbs, ¼ cup of water
- Combine all ingredients, form into balls, bake on aluminum foil lined baking sheet at 350 degrees until brown, stir into sauce and simmer for 4 hours

Brown boneless pork chops in olive oil and allow to simmer with the meatballs and sauce. Your sauce will be good if it has a golden shimmer when you look at it from the side!

Andrew and Catherine Riotto, Married May 28, 1955
Nanny and Pop Pop raised 5 children in Palo Alto, Pennsylvania. They loved to cook, eat, and to entertain their friends and family. My Nanny inspired my love of cooking and her best dish is meatballs and sauce!

Jimmy & Son's Salvage Yard, Palo Alto
Founded and Owned by Vincenzo Riotto, Andrew Riotto, & Dominic Riotto

Seafood Bisque [27]
- 1 stick of butter, ¼ cup of flour, 1 box of chicken broth, 4 cups of half and half, 1/3 cup of water, ¼ cup of diced sun dried tomatoes, 12 ounces of cod, 1 pound of peeled and deveined shrimp, ¼ cup pesto sauce, salt and pepper
- Melt butter, stir in flour, stir in liquid ingredients until incorporated, add remaining ingredients, and simmer until seafood is cooked

Lobster Macaroni and Cheese
- 2 lobster tails (cooked and diced), 1 box of elbow noodles (boiled), 4 tablespoons of flour, 4 tablespoons of butter, ½ pound of American cheese, ½ pound of gruyere cheese, 5 cups of milk, salt and pepper
- Melt butter, stir in flour, stir in milk, stir in cheeses, salt and pepper, toss with elbow noodles and lobster, and bake at 375 degrees for 15 minutes

Pork Loin [22]
- 3 pound pork loin, ½ teaspoon of garlic powder, ½ teaspoon of ginger, ½ teaspoon of thyme, salt and pepper, 2 cups of chicken broth, 2 tablespoons of lemon juice, 1 tablespoon of soy sauce
- Sprinkle dry seasonings over pork loin, brown on all sides, place into crock pot, add remaining ingredients, and cook on low for 8 hours

Chili
- 1 ½ pounds of ground beef (cooked and drained), 1 green pepper (diced), 1 red pepper (diced), 1 red onion (diced), 2 jalapenos (diced), 8 ounces of mushrooms (sliced), 1 can of dark red kidney beans (rinsed and drained), 1 can of stewed tomatoes, 2 tablespoons of chili powder, 1 cup of ketchup, 1 ½ tablespoons of lemon juice, 2 tablespoons of brown sugar, 1 tablespoon of Worcestershire sauce, 1 teaspoon of apple cider vinegar, 1 teaspoon of mustard, 1 teaspoon of cumin, 1 cup of v8
- Combine all ingredients in crock pot and cook on low for 4 hours

BBQ Chicken
- 3 teaspoons of garlic (minced and sautéed in 1 tablespoon of butter), 1 cup of ketchup, ¼ cup of brown sugar, ¼ cup of chili sauce, 2 tablespoons of Worcestershire sauce, 1 tablespoon of mustard, ½ teaspoon of hot sauce, 1 tablespoon of honey
- Combine all ingredients, simmer for 15 minutes, and brush on chicken while grilling

Crab Cakes
- 1 pound of lump crab meat, 2 tablespoons of butter, ¼ cup of red pepper (diced), ¼ cup of celery (diced), ¼ cup of onion (diced), ¼ cup of green onions (diced), ½ cup of bread crumbs, ¼ cup of mayonnaise, 1 egg (beaten), 2 tablespoons of parsley, 2 teaspoons of Worcestershire sauce, 2 teaspoons of lemon juice, 2 teaspoons of old bay seasoning, 1 teaspoon of ground mustard, ¼ teaspoon of tabasco sauce, salt and pepper

- Sauté vegetables in butter until tender, combine all ingredients, form into patties, refrigerate for 3 hours, and broil for 4 minutes per side

Shrimp Scampi

- 2 tablespoons of butter, 2 tablespoons of olive oil, 4 teaspoons of minced garlic, ¼ cup of dry white wine, 1/3 cup of chopped fresh parsley, 1 tablespoon of lemon juice, 2 pounds of peeled and deveined shrimp, salt and pepper
- Melt butter, stir in remaining ingredients, simmer until shrimp is cooked, and toss with pasta

Creamy Shrimp Pasta [18]

- 2 tablespoons of butter, 2 tablespoons of olive oil, 1 onion (diced), 2 teaspoons of minced garlic, ½ cup of white wine. 1 can of tomato sauce, 1 cup of heavy cream, ¼ cup of parsley, 6 basil leaves (torn), 1 pound of peeled and deveined shrimp, salt and pepper
- Sauté shrimp in butter and olive oil until cooked, remove from pan, stir in remaining ingredients, and toss with shrimp and pasta

Beef Noodle Soup
- 1 pound of beef cubes (lightly browned), 2 beef bouillon cubes, 3 boxes of beef broth, 1 onion, 3 carrots (peeled and diced), 3 ribs of celery, 1 bag of egg noodles (cooked)
- Combine all ingredients (except egg noodles), simmer for 25 minutes, discard onion and celery, and stir in egg noodles

Easter Pie [10]
- 3 pounds of Ricotta cheese, 2 pounds of hard salami (ground), 1 pounds of pepperoni (sliced), 6 eggs (hard boiled and diced), 4 raw eggs, ¾ cup of pecorino romano cheese
- Combine all ingredients, pour into a pie pan lined with dough, cover with dough, brush with beaten egg, and bake for 45 minutes at 350 degrees

Pottsville Grammar School (taken by S. Cicero)
Dedicated in 1865, the Pottsville Grammar School is one of the oldest buildings in Pottsville. It was utilized as Centre Street Elementary until the 1980's, [13]

City Chicken
- 2 pounds of boneless pork (cubed), 3 eggs (beaten), 3 tablespoons of milk, 2 cups of Italian seasoned bread crumbs, ¼ cup of parmesan cheese, 2 cups of water, vegetable oil, seasoned salt and pepper
- Skewer pork (3 pieces per skewer) sprinkle with seasoned salt and pepper
- Combine eggs and milk, combine Italian seasoned bread crumbs and parmesan cheese

- Dip skewers in egg mixture, dip skewers in bread crumb mixture, fry in vegetable oil for 3 minutes per side, pour water into a baking dish with a rack on top, place skewers on rack, cover with foil, and bake for 25 minutes at 350 degrees

Bean Soup
- 1 pound of navy beans (soaked overnight and drained), 2 cups of celery (diced), 1 onion (diced), 1 potato (diced), 3 carrots (diced), 1 tablespoon of parsley, 2 pounds of ham (diced), 8 cups of water, salt and pepper
- Combine all ingredients and simmer for 25 minutes

Meatloaf [19]
- 2 pounds of ground beef, 1 packet of onion soup mix, ¾ cup of bread crumbs, 2 eggs, ¾ cup of water, ½ cup of ketchup, ¼ cup of brown sugar
- Combine ketchup and brown sugar (set aside), combine all remaining ingredients, form into loaf, spread with ketchup mixture, and bake at 350 degrees for 1 hour

Goulash
- 1 pound of elbow noodles (cooked), 1 pound of ground beef, 1 onion (diced), 1 large can of diced tomatoes, 1 can of tomato sauce, 1 tablespoon of garlic salt, 1 teaspoon of sugar, salt and pepper
- Cook ground beef and onion, drain, and combine with remaining ingredients

Ham Loaf
- Loaf: 1 pound of ground pork, 1 pound of ground ham, 2/3 cup of bread crumbs, 1/3 cup of instant tapioca, ¼ cup of milk
- Combine all ingredients and form into a loaf
- Sauce: ¼ cup of cider vinegar, ½ cup of water, ½ cup of brown sugar, 1 tablespoon of mustard, 1 tablespoon of honey
- Combine all ingredients, boil for 5 minutes, pour over loaf, and bake for 2 hours at 350 degrees

Stuffed Peppers
- 6 large green peppers (tops removed, hollowed, and boiled for 5 minutes), 1 pound of ground beef, 1 onion (diced), 16 ounce can of diced tomatoes, ½ cup of white rice (cooked), 1 teaspoon of Worcestershire sauce, 1 cup of shredded cheese, salt and pepper

- Cook ground beef and onion, drain, combine with remaining ingredients, stuff into peppers, sprinkle with cheese, cover, and bake for 30 minutes at 350 degrees

Pierogis
- Dough: 2 cups of flour, 1 egg, ½ cup of warm water, 1 teaspoon of salt, 2 tablespoons of vegetable oil
- Combine all ingredients, knead, allow to rest for 45 minutes, roll out, and cut into circles
- Filling: 1 cup of mashed potatoes, 1 cup of shredded sharp cheddar cheese
- Place 2 teaspoons of filling on each dough circle, fold over, pinch closed with a fork, and boil until tender

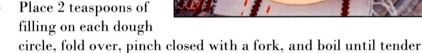

Kabobs
- 2 pounds of boneless/skinless chicken or pork (cubed), ¼ cup of dry red wine, ¼ cup of olive oil, 3 tablespoons of lemon juice, 1 small onion (grated), 1 clove of garlic (minced), 1 teaspoon of oregano, 1 teaspoon of thyme, salt and pepper
- Combine all ingredients, marinade for 3 hours, skewer with green pepper, sweet onion, and broil or grill

Grilled Bear Tenderloin [31]
- 1 pound of bear tenderloin, 1 tablespoon of vegetable oil, 1 teaspoon of salt, 1 ½ teaspoons of pepper, 1 ½ teaspoons of allspice, ¾ teaspoon of cinnamon, ¾ teaspoon of clove, ½ teaspoon of nutmeg
- Drizzle oil over tenderloin, sprinkle with seasonings, and grill

Vince Riotto with his 564 pound Black Bear, November 24, 2016

Pork and Sauerkraut
- 4 pound pork roast (sprinkled with salt/pepper and seared on all sides), 2 pounds of sauerkraut, 1.5 tablespoons of caraway seeds, 1 onion (chopped), 2 granny smith apples (peeled, cored, chopped), ½ cup of brown sugar, 1 teaspoon of paprika
- Combine all ingredients and cook on low in crock pot for 6-8 hours

Italian Steak 2
- Steaks: 3 New York strip steaks, 2 teaspoons olive oil, 2 tablespoons rosemary, 2 tablespoons thyme, 2 teaspoons of minced garlic
- Combine all ingredients and marinade for 8 hours, grill or broil
- Topping: 1 teaspoon of lemon zest, 2 teaspoons of lemon juice, 3 teaspoons of olive oil, ½ teaspoon of rosemary, 1 teaspoon of thyme, arugula, salt and pepper
- Combine all ingredients, place on top of the steaks, and top with a dippy egg

Chicken Pot Pie 33

- 3 cups of chicken (cooked and shredded), 2 quarts of chicken broth, 2 cups of flour, ½ teaspoon of baking powder, 2 tablespoons of butter (cubed), 1 cup of milk
- Combine flour, baking powder, and butter, pour in milk, knead, roll to ¼ inch thickness, cut into squares, simmer in brother for 15 minutes, stir in chicken, season with salt and pepper, and garnish with fresh parsley

Turkey Tetrazzini
- 1 tablespoon of butter, 1 onion (chopped), 2 ribs of celery (chopped), 1 cup of peas (frozen), 2 carrots (shredded), 8 ounces of mushrooms (sliced), ½ cup of white wine, ½ cup of flour, 4 cups of chicken broth, ½ cup of parmesan cheese (grated), 4 ounces of cream cheese (softened), 3 cups of turkey (shredded), 1 box of cooked pasta
- Sauté vegetables in melted butter until tender, stir in flour, stir in remaining ingredients, toss with pasta, and bake for 30-35 minutes at 350 degrees

Honey Dipped Chicken [10]

- 2 chickens (cut into serving pieces and sprinkled with salt and pepper), 1 ½ cups of flour (sifted), 1 teaspoon of baking powder, ½ teaspoon of salt, ¼ teaspoon of paprika, 1 egg, 1 cup of milk, ½ cup of honey
- Combine batter ingredients, dip chicken into batter, and deep fry until golden brown

Carbonara (shared by Sherrie Schafer)

- 3 eggs, 12 ounces of bacon (cooked and chopped), ½ cup of heavy cream, ¼ cup of milk, ¾ cup of parmesan cheese, 8 ounces of pasta (cooked)
- Combine eggs, cream, milk, parmesan, and bacon, toss with pasta, and top with bacon

Black Diamond Steak

- 2 tablespoons of olive oil, ¼ cup of soy sauce, ¼ cup of honey, 2-3 tablespoons of brown sugar, 2 tablespoons of balsamic vinegar, 1 teaspoon of ginger, ½ teaspoon of garlic powder
- Combine all ingredients, pour over steaks, and marinade overnight before grilling

Weiner Schnitzel [32]
- 4 to 8 skinless pheasant breasts or boar loan medallions, 1 cup of flour, 2 eggs (beaten), 1 cup of Italian seasoned bread crumbs
- Pound meat to ¼ inch thick, dredge meat in flour, egg, then breadcrumb, pain fry until golden brown, and sprinkle with salt and pepper

J. Reiner with her boar, January 17, 2015

Guinness Stew, [40]
- 2 ½ pounds of cubed beef (lightly browned and drained), 4 cloves of minced garlic, 2 onions (chopped), 7 slices of bacon (cooked and crumbled), 3 ½ tablespoons of flour, 1 can of Guinness, 5 tablespoon of tomato paste, 3 cups of chicken stock, 4 carrots (peeled), 2 ribs of celery (chopped), 1 parsnip (peeled and chopped), 2 bay leaves, 1 teaspoon of thyme, 1 teaspoon of coffee extract, ¼ cup of water, 3 dried prunes (diced)
- Simmer all ingredients for 2 hours, stir in 8 red potatoes (quartered), and simmer for 30-40 minutes

Desserts
Life is short, lick that bowl!

Peanut Butter Pie

- 4 ounces of cream cheese (softened), ½ cup of peanut butter, ½ cup of milk, 1 cup of powdered sugar, 1 tub of cool whip
- Combine all ingredients, pour into a graham cracker crust, and freeze

Rhubarb Pie

- 3 eggs (beaten), 3 tablespoons of milk, 1 ½ cups of sugar, ¼ cup of flour, ¾ teaspoon of nutmeg, 3 cups of rhubarb (diced), 1 cup of strawberries (diced), 1 tablespoon of instant tapioca, 1 tablespoon of butter
- Combine all ingredients, pour into a pie crust, and bake for 55 minutes at 400 degrees

Cut Out Cookies

- 1 cup of sugar, ½ teaspoon of salt, 1 cup of butter (softened), 4 ounces of cream cheese (softened), ½ teaspoon of almond extract, ½ teaspoon of vanilla extract, 1 egg yolk, 2 ¾ cups of flour
- Cream together all ingredients (except flour), add flour gradually, chill for 1 hour, roll, cutout, and bake for 7-10 minutes at 350 degrees

Thumbprint Cookies

- Cookie: 1 cup of butter (softened), 2/3 cup of sugar, ½ teaspoon of vanilla extract, 2 cups of flour
- Combine all ingredients and chill for 1 hour, shape dough into 1 inch balls, make an imprint with your thumb, fill with jam, sprinkle with sugar, and bake for 10 minutes at 350 degrees
- Glaze: 1 cup of powdered sugar, 3 teaspoons of water, 1 ½ teaspoons of almond extract
- Combine all ingredients and drizzle over cooled cookies

Chocolate Bar Cake

- 1 box chocolate cake mix (baked according to directions in a 9x13 dish), 1 tub of cool whip, 3 chocolate bars (your choice, crushed), 1 jar of caramel ice cream topping, 1 can of sweetened condensed milk
- While warm, poke holes all over cake and pour over caramel and sweetened condensed milk, allow to cool, and top with whipped cream and crushed chocolate bars

Pumpkin Pecan Pie [34]

- 3 eggs, 1 cup of dark corn syrup, ½ cup of sugar, 4 tablespoons of melted butter, 1 cup of pureed pumpkin, 1.5 teaspoons of vanilla, 1 cup of chopped pecans
- Combine all ingredients, pour into a pie crust, and bake for 60 minutes at 350 degrees

Pound Cake

- 1 cup of butter, 3 cups of sugar, 6 eggs, 3 cups of flour (sifted), ¼ teaspoon of baking soda, 8 ounces of sour cream, 2 teaspoons of vanilla extract
- Cream butter and sugar, mix in remaining ingredients, pour into a greased bundt pan, and bake for 1 ½ hours at 300 degrees

Apple Dumplings [20]

- 1 boxed pie crust, 6 granny smith apples (peeled and cored)
- Cut each pie crust into 3 sections, place an apple on each section, fill apple with sugar and cinnamon, top with a ½ teaspoon of butter, fold dough around apple, and place in a 9x13 baking dish
- Syrup: 1 cup of sugar, 2 cups of water, 3 tablespoons of butter, ½ teaspoon of cinnamon

- Combine all ingredients, boil for 3 minutes, pour over apples, and bake for 45 minutes at 425 degrees

Vanilla Crumb Pie
- Filling: ½ cup of brown sugar, 1 tablespoon of flour, ¼ cup of corn syrup, 1 cup of water, 1 egg, 2 teaspoons of vanilla
- Combine all ingredients, bring to boil, remove from heat, cool, and pour into a pie crust
- Topping: 1 cup of flour, ½ cup of brown sugar, ½ teaspoon of baking soda, ¼ cup of sugar, ¼ cup of cold butter
- Combine all ingredients until crumbled, sprinkle over filling, and bake at 350 degree for 45 minutes

CMP Cake [21]
- Crust: ½ cup of chopped peanuts, ½ cup of butter (melted), 2 cups of graham cracker crumbs
- Combine all ingredients, press into the bottom of a 9x13 pan, bake for 15 minutes at 350 degrees, and cool
- Layer 1: ½ cup of peanut butter, 1 block of cream cheese (softened), 1 cup of powdered sugar, 8 ounces of cool whip
- Combine all ingredients and spread over crust
- Layer 2: 2 boxes of chocolate pudding mix (instant), 2 ¾ cups of milk
- Combine ingredients and spread over layer 1
- Layer 3: 8 ounces of cool whip, 1 cup of marshmallow fluff
- Combine ingredients and spread over layer 2
- Top with chopped peanuts and refrigerate

This may remind you of a CMP sundae from Heisler's!

Potato Candy
- ¼ cup of mashed potatoes, 2 tablespoons of milk, 1 teaspoon of vanilla, 1 box of powdered sugar, peanut butter
- Combine all ingredients (except peanut butter), chill for 2 hours, roll out dough, spread with peanut butter, roll up, chill for 1 hour, and slice

Pumpkin Roll
- Roll: ¾ cup of flour, ½ teaspoon of baking powder, ½ teaspoon of baking soda, ½ teaspoon of cinnamon, ½ teaspoon of ground cloves, ¼ teaspoon of salt, 3 eggs, 1 cup of sugar, 2/3 cup of pureed pumpkin
- Combine all ingredients and spread onto a jelly-roll pan lined with greased and floured wax paper, bake for 15 minutes at 375 degrees, remove from the oven, and roll into a dish towel sprinkled with powdered sugar until cool

- Filling: 1 block of cream cheese, 1 cup of powdered sugar, 6 tablespoons of butter, 1 teaspoon of vanilla extract
- Combine all ingredients, unroll cake, spread filling over cake, roll, wrap in plastic, and store in the refrigerator

Ricotta Cookies
- Cookies: 2 sticks of butter (softened), 2 cups of sugar, 15 ounces of ricotta, zest of 1 lemon, 2 teaspoons of vanilla extract, 2 eggs, 4 cups of flour, 2 teaspoons of baking soda, ¾ teaspoon of salt
- Cream butter and sugar, mix in eggs and remaining ingredients, chill for 2 hours, roll into balls, drop onto parchment paper lined baking sheets, bake for 15 minutes at 350 degrees, and cool
- Glaze: 1 tablespoon of butter (melted), 4 cups of powdered sugar, 2 tablespoons of lemon juice, ¼ cup of milk, 2 teaspoons of vanilla extract
- Combine all ingredients, spread over cookies, and sprinkle with jimmies

Banana Cream Pie (shared by D. Riotto)
- ½ cup of milk, 1 cup of sour cream, 1 package of vanilla pudding, 1 tub of cool whip, 3 bananas (sliced)
- Combine all ingredients, spread half into the bottom of a graham cracker crust, top with bananas, spread remaining over bananas, and refrigerate

Butterscotch Fudge
- 1 can of sweetened condensed milk, 1 package of butterscotch chips, 1 ½ cups of miniature marshmallows, 2/3 cup of peanut butter, 1 teaspoon of vanilla extract, 1 cup of chopped peanuts
- Combine all ingredients, melt in microwave, pour into a 9x13 baking dish sprayed with non-stick spray, and refrigerate

Candied Nuts
- 1 cup of sugar, 1 teaspoon of cinnamon, 1 teaspoon of salt, 1 egg white (beaten), 1 tablespoon of water, 1 pound of pecans or almonds
- Combine all ingredients and bake for 1 hour at 250 degrees (toss every 15 minutes)

Molasses Candy
- ½ cup of dark brown sugar, 1 ½ cups of molasses, 1 tablespoon of butter, 1 tablespoon of vinegar, 1 teaspoon of baking soda
- Combine all ingredients (except baking soda) and boil until a drop forms a hard ball in ice water, stir in baking soda and pour into a greased 8 inch baking dish, cool, and break into pieces

Rice Pudding
- ¾ cup of white rice (cooked), 2 cups of milk, 1/3 cup of white sugar, ¼ teaspoon of salt, 1 egg (beaten), 2/3 cup of raisins, 1 tablespoon of butter, ¾ teaspoon of vanilla extract
- Combine all ingredients (except egg, ½ cup of milk, and vanilla), simmer over medium heat until thick, stir in milk, egg, and vanilla

Pottsville (submitted by S. Cicero)

Centre and Mahantongo Streets, Pottsville (submitted by S. Cicero)

Polish Angel Wings 28
- 5 tablespoons of heavy cream, 5 egg yolks, ½ teaspoon salt, ¼ cup of sugar, 2 ¼ cups of flour, 1 teaspoon of vanilla
- Combine all ingredients, knead, allow to rest for 20 minutes, knead, roll out, cut into 1x4 inch rectangles, fry in vegetable oil until golden, drain on paper towels, and dust with powdered sugar

Kiffles 30
- Cookies: 2 ¼ cups of flour, ½ teaspoon of salt, 1 block of cream cheese (softened), 1 cup of butter (softened)
- Combine cream cheese and butter, stir in remaining ingredients, chill dough for 2 hours, roll out, and cut into 2 inch squares
- Place a spoon of jam onto each square, pinch opposite corners of dough together, bake on parchment lined cookie sheet for 14 minutes at 375 degrees, cool, and dust with powdered sugar

Nut Tocci 3
- Cookies: 1 cup of butter, 2 blocks of cream cheese, 2 cups of flour
- Combine all ingredients (except flour), stir in flour, and press into the bottom and up the sides of mini muffin cups
- Filling: combine 1 ½ cups of brown sugar, ½ cups of egg whites, 2 tablespoons of butter (melted), 1 teaspoon of vanilla extract, 1 ¼ cups of chopped pecans
- Place 2 teaspoons of filling into each cookie cup and bake for 20 minutes at 350 degrees

Maraschino Cherry and Walnut Cake 10
- 1 yellow cake mix, 1 vanilla instant pudding mix, ½ cup of vegetable oil, ½ cup of water, ½ cup of Four Queens whiskey, 5 eggs, 1 cup od chopped walnuts, 1 jar of maraschino cherries (10 ounces, chopped and undrained)
- Combine all ingredients, pour into greased bundt pan, bake for 60 minutes at 350 degrees, and dust with powdered sugar

Gumdrop Bread [10]

- 2 ½ cups of flour 1 ¼ cups of buttermilk, ½ cup of sugar, ½ cup of brown sugar, ¼ cup of shortening, 2 eggs, 1 teaspoon of salt, 3 teaspoons of baking powder, 1 teaspoon of vanilla, ½ teaspoons of baking soda, 1 ¼ cups of gum drops (chopped)
- Combine all ingredients, pour into a greased loaf pan, and bake for 60 minutes at 350 degrees

Nut Roll [10]

- Dough: 2 ounces of cake yeast, ¼ cup of water (warm), 6 eggs, 16 ounces of sour cream, 16 ounces of butter, 1 cup of sugar, 1 teaspoon of vanilla extract, ½ teaspoon salt, 10 cups of flour
- Combine yeast and water, stir in remaining ingredients (except flour), gradually add in flour, separate into 8 pieces, and roll each piece into a 9x14 rectangle

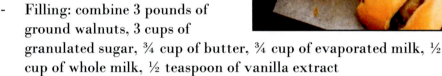

- Filling: combine 3 pounds of ground walnuts, 3 cups of granulated sugar, ¾ cup of butter, ¾ cup of evaporated milk, ½ cup of whole milk, ½ teaspoon of vanilla extract
- Spread filling evenly over each piece of dough, roll up, allow to rest for 3 hours, and bake for 20 minutes at 350 degrees (bake 2 rolls per sheet at a time)

Italian Coffee Cake [10]

- 1 cup of shortening, 1 cup of sugar, 4 eggs, 4 cups of flour, 4 teaspoons of baking powder, zest of 1 lemon, juice of 1 lemon, 1 cup of milk, 1 teaspoon of anisette extract, 1 teaspoon of vanilla extract
- Combine flour and baking powder, in a separate bowl combine shortening, sugar, eggs, extracts, juice, zest, and gradually mix in dry ingredients, alternating with milk
- Pour into a greased bundt pan and bake for 45 minutes at 350 degrees

Shoo-fly Pie
- Crumb topping: 1 ½ cups of flour, ½ cup of dark brown sugar, 1 teaspoon of cinnamon, ½ teaspoon of nutmeg, ⅛ teaspoon of salt, 1 stick of butter (cold)
- Combine all ingredients until crumbly
- Filling: ¾ cup of molasses, ¾ cup of boiling water, ½ teaspoon of baking soda
- Combine all ingredients, pour into pie crust, top with crumb topping, and bake for 40 minutes at 350 degrees

Sticky Buns
- Dough: 1 cup of milk (warmed), 2 teaspoons of yeast, 2 teaspoons of salt, 2 eggs (beaten), ¼ cup of honey, ½ cup of butter (melted), 3 ½ cups of flour
- Combine all ingredients (except flour), stir in flour, allow to rest for 4 hours, roll into a 20 inch rectangle
- Topping: ¾ cup of butter (melted), 1 ¼ cups of brown sugar, 1/3 cup of honey, 1 teaspoon of cinnamon, ½ teaspoon of salt, 2 cups of pecans (chopped)
- Combine all ingredients and spread ¼ on the bottom of a 9 inch cake pan, top with dough, spread remaining topping over dough, roll up dough, slice into 9 pieces, allow to rest for 1 hour, lay in greased baking dish, and bake for 40 minutes at 350 degrees

Fry Bread
- 2 cups of flour, 3 teaspoons of baking powder, 1 teaspoon of salt, 1 cup of milk
- Stir dry ingredients, lightly stir in milk, knead dough, shape into disks, fry at 375 degrees until golden, and dust with powdered sugar

Zucchini Cake
- 3 cups of flour, 1 ½ teaspoon of baking soda, 1 ½ teaspoon of salt, ¾ teaspoon of baking powder, 1 teaspoon of cinnamon, 4 egg, 2 cups of sugar, 1 cup of oil, 1 teaspoon of vanilla, 2 cups of zucchini (shredded), 1 cup of raisins, 1 cup of walnuts (chopped)
- Combine all ingredients beginning with sugar, oil, and eggs
- Pour into 2 greased loaf pans and bake for 45 minutes at 350 degrees

Whoopie Pies
- Cakes: 2 cups of sugar, 1 cup of vegetable oil, 2 eggs, 4 cups of flour, 1 cup of cocoa, 1 teaspoon of salt, 1 cup of buttermilk, 2 teaspoons of vanilla, 2 teaspoons of baking soda, 1 cup of water (hot)
- Combine sugar, vegetable oil, and eggs, stir in dry ingredients alternating with buttermilk and hot water, drop by spoonful onto greased baking sheet, bake for 8-10 minutes at 350 degrees, and cool

- Filling: 1 cup of butter (softened), 2 ¾ cups of powdered sugar, 4 cups of marshmallow fluff, 2 teaspoons of vanilla
- Combine all ingredients until fluffy and spread between 2 cakes

Wine Cookies [10]
- 1 cup of vegetable oil, 1 cup of red wine, 2 sticks of cinnamon, 3 cloves ¼ teaspoon of salt, flour
- Combine all ingredients (except for the four) and bring to boil for 5-8 minutes, cool, and stir in flour until dough forms
- Shape into balls or shells, bake on a greased cookie sheet at 400 degrees until lightly browned, and drizzle with and honey

Doughnut Muffins 10
- 1 3/4 cups of flour, 1 ½ teaspoons of baking powder, ½ teaspoon of salt, ½ teaspoon of nutmeg, ¼ teaspoon of cinnamon, ¾ cup of sugar, 1/3 cup of vegetable oil, 1 egg (beaten), ¾ cup of milk, jelly
- Combine all ingredients, pour into lined muffin cups (fill halfway, top with jam, and cover with batter), bake for 20 minutes at 350 degrees, and top with additional cinnamon, sugar, and melted butter

Carrot and Molasses Muffins 10
- 1 egg (beaten), 1 cup of bran cereal, 2 carrots (shredded), ½ cup of plain yogurt, ½ cup of tomato juice, ½ teaspoon of salt, ½ cup of molasses, ¼ cup of vegetable oil, 1 cup of wheat flour, 1 ½ cups of flour, 1 ½ teaspoon of baking soda
- Combine all ingredients, pour into lined muffin pans, and bake for 18 minutes at 400 degrees

Nut Horns 10
- Dough: ½ pound of butter (softened), 3 cups of flour (sifted), 3 egg yolks (beaten), 1 tablespoon of sugar, 8 tablespoons of evaporated milk, 1 teaspoon of vanilla, 1 small cake yeast, ¼ cup of water (warm)
- Dissolve yeast and sugar in water, stir in milk, combine flour, butter, egg yolks, yeast mixture, and kneed until smooth
- Filling: combine ground walnuts, 3 egg whites (beaten), 1 ½ cups of sugar
- Roll dough into balls, roll out each ball on a board dusted with powdered sugar, put a small amount of filling on each, fold and shape into crescents, and bake for 15-20 minutes at 375 degrees

Teaberry Ice Cream
- ¾ cup of milk, 1/3 cup of sugar, 1/3 cup of heavy cream, 3 drops of teaberry candy oil, 3 drops of pink gel food coloring
- Combine all ingredients and freeze in ice cream maker

Nut Clusters
- 1 pound of salted peanuts, 1 pound of unsalted peanuts, 1 bag of semi-sweet chocolate chips, 6 ounces of German's sweet chocolate, 2.5 pounds of almond bark
- Place all ingredients into crock pot and cook on low until melted (about 1-2 hours), stir to combine, and drop by spoonful into cupcake liners

Coconut Eggs
- 8 ounces of cream cheese (softened), 1 tablespoon of margarine (softened), 1 cup of shredded coconut, 1 pound of powdered sugar
- Cream the margarine and cream cheese, stir in remaining ingredients, shape into eggs, and dip in melted chocolate

Peanut Butter Eggs
- 3 pounds of powdered sugar, ¾ pound of butter (softened), 1 large container peanut butter
- Cream all ingredients, shape into eggs, and dip in melted chocolate

Molasses Eggs
- 8 ounces of cream cheese (softened), 1 tablespoon of margarine (softened), 1 ½ cups of shredded coconut, 3 tablespoons of molasses, 1 pound of powdered sugar
- Cream all ingredients, chill, shape into eggs, and dip in melted chocolate

For the Furry Ones
I bet the humans tell us that chocolate will kill us so they can eat it all!

Frozen Watermelon Treats, 35
- 1 quarter of a watermelon (pureed), 1 can of coconut milk
- Blend ingredients until smooth and freeze in ice cube trays until firm

Peanut Butter and Bacon Donuts, 36
- 1 cup of flour, 1 cup of oats, 1/3 cup of coconut oil, ½ cup of peanut butter, 2 eggs
- Combine all ingredients, press into a donut pan, bake at 375 degrees for 15 minutes, cool, and top with Greek yogurt and crumbled bacon

Banana and Peanut Butter Treats, 37
- 1 ½ cups of oats, 1 banana, ½ cup of peanut butter
- Combine all ingredients, roll dough to ¼ inch thickness, cut into bone shapes, and bake at 350 degrees for 15 minutes

Catnip Treats, 38
- 5 ounces of tuna (drained), 1 egg, ½ cup of flour, ¼ cup of wheat germ, ½ cup of cornmeal, ¼ cup of wheat four, ¼ cup of water, 1 tablespoon of catnip
- Combine all ingredients, roll to ½ inch thickness, cut into fish shapes, and bake at 350 degrees for 20 minutes

Tuna Crackers, 39
- 6 ounces of tuna, 1 cup of cornmeal, 1 cup of wheat flour, 1/3 cup of water
- Combine all ingredients, roll into balls, flatten, and bake at 350 degrees for 20 minutes

Sammy and Cookie Reiner

Recipes Inspired By and Adapted From

1. Taste of Home, https://www.tasteofhome.com/recipes/bourbon-candied-bacon-deviled-eggs
2. Giada De Laurentiis, http://www.foodnetwork.com/recipes/giada-de-laurentiis/strawberry-bruschetta-recipe-1941838
3. 2007 Family Cookbook, Wal-Mart
4. Ina Garten, http://www.foodnetwork.com/recipes/ina-garten/easy-cheese-board-3539085
5. SBC Canning, http://www.sbcanning.com/2011/10/canning-flavor-of-harry-and-davids.html
6. Comfortable Food, http://comfortablefood.com/spicy-bread-and-butter-pickles/
7. Canning Confessions, http://www.canningconfessions.com/2011/10/cowboy-candy-texas-taste-teaser.html
8. The Vintage Cook, http://clientwp.mywebproof.net/scrapple/
9. Simply Recipes, http://www.simplyrecipes.com/recipes/corned_beef_hash/
10. The Great Radio Cookbook, Great Radio 141- WLSH Lansford, Great Radio 145 – WPAM, Pottsville
11. Banshee Sports, http://www.bansheesports.net/2014/09/cooking-with-banshee-coal-region-hot.html
12. Food Family Finds, http://foodfamilyfinds.com/end-of-summer-caramel-apple-sangria-recipe-mirassousummer/
13. Trisha Yearwood, http://www.foodnetwork.com/recipes/trisha-yearwood/bpt-bacon-pimiento-and-tomato-sandwich-2545242
14. All Recipes, http://allrecipes.com/recipe/221982/slow-cooked-collard-greens/
15. All Recipes, http://allrecipes.com/recipe/34342/easter-cheese---hrudka/
16. All Recipes, http://allrecipes.com/recipe/7042/paska-bread/
17. Recipescool, http://recipescool.com/french-onion-soup-casserole/
18. Ree Drummond, http://www.foodnetwork.com/recipes/ree-drummond/penne-alla-betsy-recipe-2127651
19. Lipton, http://www.liptonkitchens.com/recipes/detail/9252/1/souperior-meatloaf
20. Taste of Home, https://www.tasteofhome.com/recipes/easy-apple-dumplings
21. QVC, http://www.qvc.com/CMPCake.content.html
22. Trisha Yearwood, http://flavorite.net/2016/01/30/trisha-yearwoods-crock-pot-pork-loin/
23. Key Ingredient, https://www.keyingredient.com/recipes/867105080/ham-cheese-sticky-buns/
24. Big Oven, https://www.bigoven.com/recipe/american-cheese-sauce/630440
25. Damn Delicious, http://damndelicious.net/2014/11/19/easy-green-bean-casserole/
26. All Recipes, http://allrecipes.com/recipe/13743/pennsylvania-dutch-pickled-beets-and-eggs/
27. Betty Crocker, https://www.bettycrocker.com/recipes/seafood-bisque/f12178a7-a396-43c1-9d31-0b6d6e7b03dc
28. Food, http://www.food.com/recipe/polish-angel-wings-chrusciki-359778
29. Cooking Quotes, Pinterest (various), http://www.pinterest.com
30. Food 52, http://food52.com/recipes/66664-polish-kiffles

31. New Jersey Division of Fish and Wildlife, http://nj.gov.dep/fgw/pdg/near.recipeguide.pdf
32. Honest Food, http://honest-food.net/wild-game/wild-pig-recipes/
33. The Country Cook, http://www.thecountrycook.net/old-fashioned-chicken-and-dumplings/
34. Genius Kitchen, http://www/geniuskitchen/com/amp/recipe/paula-deens-pumpkin-pecan-pie-266260
35. Grrfeisty, http://www.grrfeisty.com/2016/06/watermelon-pupsicles.html
36. Sunny Day Family, http://www.sunnydayfamily.com/2017/01/dog-donuts.html?m=1
37. Munchkins and the Military, http://www.munchkinsandmilitary.com/2015/02/homemade-peanut-butter-banana-dog-treats.html
38. Mess for Less, http://www.messforless.net/catnip-cat-treats-recipe/?
39. ASPCA, http://www.aspcapetinsurance.com/blog/2015/august/17/3-simple-homemade-cat-treats-recipes/?pp=1
40. Chunky Chef, https://www.thechunkychef.com/guinness-coffee-irish-beef-stew/

Photo Caption Sources

1. The Morning Call, http://www.mcall.com/news/nationworld/pennsylvania/mc-pa-last-coal-breaker-20150528-story.html
2. Department of Conservation and National Resources, http://www.dcnr.pa.gov/StateParks/FindAPark/TuscaroraStatePark/Pages/default.aspx
3. Sweet Arrow Lake Park, http://www.sweetarrowlakepark.com/History.html
4. Centralia, http://www.centraliapa.org/abandoned-centralia-old-route-61/
5. USA Today, https://www.usatoday.com/story/money/personalfinance/2013/12/01/yuengling-pennsylvania-beer-brewery/3654607/
6. Interesting Pennsylvania and Beyond, http://www.interestingpennsylvania.com/2017/04/schuylkill-county-covered-bridges-rock.html?m=1
7. Civil War Blog, http://civilwar.gratzpa.org/2011/09/soldiers-monument-of-schuylkill-county-proposal/
8. Pottsville in the Twentieth Century, https://books.google.com/books?id=G2oTA3NMxwEC&printsec=frontcover&dq=inauthor:%22Mark+T.+Major%22&hl=en&sa=X&ved=0ahUKEwjNwbacxcXWAhULOCYKHQXlA0sQ6AEIMTAC#v=onepage&q&f=false
9. Republican Herald, http://m.republicanherald.com/news/lofty-tunnel-a-leftover-ghost-of-anthracite-heyday-1.1628174
10. SCMA, http://www.scmawater.com/about-us/
11. Joseph Henry Zerbe Historical Society, reported by Stephen Pytak http://republicanherald.com/news/tunnels-beneath-former-ywca-building-attract-curiosity-1.1191158
12. Flickr, https://www.flickr.com/photos/clyde239/6728350545
13. Republican Herald, http://m.republicanherald.com/news/historical-society-to-celebrate-150th-anniversary-of-grammar-school-in-pottsville-1.1935772

Thank You

Dr. Harold Aurand, History

Mr. & Mrs. Shawn Cicero, Photography

Jennifer Walser, Editing and Design

R. Thomas Berner, Editing and Design

Thank you, your efforts are greatly appreciated!

United States Department of Agriculture Safe Minimum Internal Temperature Chart

Cook all food to these minimum internal temperatures as measured with a food thermometer before removing food from the heat source.

Beef, Pork Veal, Lamb	145 Degrees Fahrenheit, rest for 3 minutes
Ground Meats	160 Degrees Fahrenheit
Ham (fully cooked)	USDA inspected – 140 Degrees Fahrenheit, Inspected by all others – 165 Degrees Fahrenheit
Poultry	165 Degrees Fahrenheit
Eggs	160 Degrees Fahrenheit
Fish and Shellfish	145 Degrees Fahrenheit

Measurements

Cup	Ounces	Tablespoon	Teaspoon
1	8	16	48
3/4	6	12	36
2/3	5 1/3	10.6	32
1/2	4	8	24
1/3	2 2/3	5.3	16
1/4	2	4	12
1/8	1	2	6
1/16	1/2	1	3

Index

Apple Cider Boilo	27
Apple Dumplings	63
Apple or Pear Butter	17
Apple Sangria	27
Apples and Cranberries	43
Bacon and Swiss Dip	10
Bacon Wrapped Water Chestnuts	9
Baked German Potato Salad	37
Balsamic Dressing	24
Banana and Peanut Butter Pet Treats	75
Banana Cream Pie	65
BBQ	31
BBQ Chicken	50
Bean Soup	54
Beef Noodle Soup	52
Beer and Cheddar Dip	10
Black Diamond Steak	59
Bleenies	11
Boilo	26
Bow Tie Pasta Salad	39
Bread Bowl Spinach Dip	11
Broccoli Salad	39
Brown Sugar Glazed and Stuffed Burgers	33
Buffalo Chicken Dip	9
Butterscotch Fudge	66
Caesar Dressing	24
Candied Jalapenos	18
Candied Nuts	66
Carbonara	59
Carrot and Molasses Muffins	72
Catnip Pet Treats	75
Cheese Ball	11
Cheese Board	12
Chicken Noodle Soup	46
Chicken Pot Pie	58
Chili	50
Chow Chow	21

City Chicken	54
CMP Cake	64
Coconut Eggs	73
Colcannon	40
Collard Greens	39
Corn Cob Jelly	21
Crab Cakes	50
Crab Stuffed Mushrooms	12
Creamed Cucumbers	43
Creamy Shrimp Pasta	51
Cut Out Cookies	62
Dandelion Jelly	17
Doughnut Muffins	72
Easter Pie	52
Filling	35
French Onion Casserole	41
Frozen Watermelon Pet Treats	75
Fry Bread	70
Goulash	55
Green Bean Casserole	36
Green Beans and Tomatoes	40
Grilled Bear Tenderloin	57
Guiness Stew	60
Gumdrop Bread	69
Halupki	45
Halushki	45
Ham and Cheese Sticky Buns	30
Ham Loaf	55
Hamburger and Hot Dog Chili Sauce	24
Hash	19
Hash Brown Casserole	40
Heath Bar Cake	63
Honey Dipped Chicken	59
Honey Glazed Carrots	37
Horseradish and Red Beet Sauce	26
Hot Bacon Dressing	26
Hot Bologna	17
Hrudka (Easter Cheese)	41
Irish Pub Cheese	12
Italian Coffee Cake	69

Italian Steak	58
Kabobs	56
Kiffles	68
Lobster Cheesesteak	31
Lobster Macaroni and Cheese	49
Macaroni and Cheese	46
Macaroni Salad	36
Maple Bacon Deviled Eggs	10
Maraschino Cherry and Walnut Cake	68
Meatballs and Sauce	47
Meatloaf	54
Molasses Candy	66
Molasses Eggs	73
Mushroom Bruschetta	14
Nut Clusters	73
Nut Horns	72
Nut Roll	69
Nut Tocci	68
Paska	43
Peanut Butter Bacon Pet Donuts	75
Peanut Butter Eggs	73
Peanut Butter Pie	62
Pierogis	56
Pimento Cheese, Bacon, and Fried Tomato Sandwiches	33
Pineapple Bake	40
Pizza Hot Sauce	26
Polish Angel Wings	68
Pork and Sauerkraut	57
Pork Loin	49
Potato Candy	64
Potato Salad	37
Pound Cake	63
Pumpkin Pecan Pie	63
Pumpkin Roll	65
Ramen Slaw	36
Red Beet Eggs	39
Red Sangria	27
Rhubard Custard Pie	62
Rhubard Jam	21
Rice Pudding	66

Ricotta Cookies	65
Roasted Brussels Sprouts	35
Sausage and Peppers	30
Scrappel	19
Seafood Bisque	49
Shoo fly Pie	70
Shrimp Scampi	51
Spinach and Water Chestnut Dip	9
Stewed Burgers	30
Sticky Buns	70
Strawberry Bruschetta	14
Stuffed Peppers	55
Sweet and Spicy Pickles	18
Sweet Pepper Relish	18
Taco Dip	9
Teaberry Ice Cream	73
Thumbprint Cookies	62
Traditional Bruschetta	14
Traditional Cole Slaw	41
Tuna Pet Cracker	75
Turkey Tetrazzini	58
Vanilla Crumb Pie	64
Weiner Schnitzel	60
White Sangria	27
Whoopie Pies	71
Wine Cookies	71
Zucchini Cake	71

Made in the USA
Middletown, DE
28 December 2017